The
Broke Man's
Survival Guide

50 Simple Strategies To Use When You Are Unemployed, Underpaid OR Just Dead Broke And trying to survive!

By A.M. Harris

AMHAR Publications

FOR ADDITIONAL COPIES VISIT:

WWW.THEBROKEMANSURVIVALGUIDE.COM

OR WRTIE:

AMHAR PUBLICATIONS

20650 S. CICERO AVE, UNIT 735

MATTESON, IL 60443

This book is dedicated to my mom. Thanks, Mom, for all of your love, support, and encouragement and for teaching me how to survive. I would also like to thank my friends and family for encouraging me through this project. A final thanks to the hardworking people who inspired me to write this guide and allowed me to document their experiences.

Table of Contents

SECTION II
SURVIVING LIFE'S LITTLE SETBACKS............**85**

A Note from the Author

I 've worked as a program director for a large non-profit organization for more than twenty-five years, helping to provide much-needed emergency services to the downtrodden, unemployed, and underemployed. I spearheaded programs at the organization that included job placement services, and emergency assistance for utility disconnections, pending evictions, and foreclosures.

Many of our clients lost jobs they held for twenty years or more. Before coming to us, many of them had been out-of-work for several months. Although we were able to help some clients find new jobs that were comparable to the salary they lost, many, many others did not find an equivalent job and were forced to settle for mediocre, low paying jobs just to keep food on the table and regularly faced the possibility of utility shut-offs and eviction.

As the program director, it was my responsibility to develop life skills and training programs to help these families get back on track. Clients needed to know how to make ends meet and the one size fits all approach found in most resource materials didn't offer the dead-on solutions clients needed. In most cases, people just want to know what they have to do to survive and make it another day without the red tape and politically correct mumbo jumbo that comes along with the territory. Sometimes the best way to help people is to "tell them like it is" and give them just right ideas and point them in just the right direction.

In this book, I've captured the very best of years' worth of front-line solutions offering 50 simple, realistic topics to help people deal with difficult issues. It is my intention to give people who are just about at rock bottom the on- target, hard hitting tactics they need to deal with real life issues that range from keeping food on the table and avoiding eviction to getting rid of a deadbeat boyfriend.

Introduction
"Ode to the Broke Man"

================

Millions of people are out of work. Unemployment is on the rise and many who are employed are having trouble making ends meet because they are not earning a decent wage.

The number of people who are losing or have lost their homes to foreclosure is staggering. So, the last thing they want to hear about are saving plans, financial portfolios, or investment strategies. They are broke! Debt collectors are calling. Disconnection notices are mounting. Foreclosure is pending. They want to hear about how they are going to make it. Real talk. How are they going to survive through it?

The Broke Man's Survival Guide answers that question by offering real-life options to consider when you literally don't have two nickels to rub together.

The fifty simple strategies covered in this guide were compiled after speaking to several former "broke enthusiasts" who have weathered the storm of job lay-offs, unemployment, chronic illness, student loans, or just unwise choices. They all survived and so can you.

This guide is divided into two sections: 1) *Surviving The Debt Pool*, which focuses on debt traps the broke man is susceptible to, debt collectors and juggling past due debt; 2) *Surviving Life's Little Setbacks*, which focuses on ways to survive the hard times in life.

So, instead of worrying about things that are beyond your control at the moment, let's learn how to survive through it!

Section I
Surviving the Debt Pool

S ometimes in life, there are unforeseen circumstances that come out of nowhere. Let us not forget the infamous Enron scandal of 2002, where thousands of employees lost their jobs and benefits as a result of the scandal that caused the corporate giant to file bankruptcy. I am sure many Enron employees woke up that historic morning prepared for a normal day at the office and were devastated to discover they were without a job.

Many "dispensable" workers were escorted from the building by security while others were fired at home via phone messages. Perhaps one of them had just purchased a new home a month prior, or purchased a new car the weekend before, thinking that they could easily foot the bills with their safe and sound Enron salary. Then suddenly, without warning, they are fired and given a measly $4,500 severance package, devoid of any consideration of their many years of service to the company.

Undoubtedly, some of these former Enron employees were forced to start a new job earning a pay rate that did not match the salary it took years for them to build at Enron. This lower pay rate probably didn't make ends meet in the lifestyle they had grown accustomed to. Worst of all, many former Enron employees, who had paid their bills on time for years, may have found themselves hastily pulled into the downward spiral of debt.

The downward spiral starts with being forced to pay only the minimum amount due on credit card bills to assure that there is enough money to pay the most important bills, like the mortgage and the car note. Next, the minimum payments are paid late, and then they are not paid at all. Soon the car note falls behind because the mortgage has to be paid. Before they knew it, the phone was ringing off the hook from angry debt collectors who have never called before, complaining about the late bills.

Okay, in the beginning your creditors are considerate and courteous, especially if there has been a good payment history. However, it won't take long for those pleasant creditors to become impatient and cruel. Suddenly, you are labeled as one of those "deadbeat bill dodgers," who has no interest in paying down the accumulated debt and is swiftly turned over to their collections department.

In this book, Strategies 1-23 makes a case for people who find themselves caught up in a credit system that rates them as good or bad without consideration of their individual circumstances: a system that adores you when you can pay your bills but destroys you when you cannot and enacts punishments that do not always fit the crime. For instance, many lenders would rather foreclose on your home of twenty years and auction it off for pennies on the dollars than give you the opportunity to refinance at a more affordable rate.

Millions of honest people get trapped in circumstances that are beyond their control due to unemployment, divorce, or illness. There should be some type of mercy and compassion for them.

Nearly 90 percent of bankruptcies occur because of illness, lost job, or divorce and are not the result of haphazard credit use. This calculates into thousands of honest folks who, despite many years of paying their bills on time, find themselves thrust in the sea of endless debt. And despite the fact that they would pay their bills in a heartbeat (if they had the money), they are hounded and harassed by debt collectors like the "deadbeats" they are not.

Although some of the strategies detail ways to avoid debt collectors, this is not an attempt to downplay the fact that you owe your creditors money and encourage you not to pay your bills. Nor are they designed to help you live carelessly or irresponsibly. If you are able to pay your bills, then by all means PAY THEM!

However, if you are unable to pay your bills — I mean no way, no how — and all obvious methods of financial survival has been exhausted *(your savings are gone, unemployment has run out, your attempts to reason with creditors have failed and you are living paycheck-to-paycheck)*, then I hope this guide provides you with information that might help you devise a survival plan before the worst happens (foreclosure, bankruptcy, wage garnishment, or vehicle repossession). If the worst has already happened, then I hope the following strategies can help you weather the storm.

Strategy #1
Hang Up!

For the life of me, I cannot understand why people think they have to stay on the phone and listen to a rude debt collector! They sit there, endlessly trying to plead their case—struggling to explain to an apathetic debt collector the reasons they have been unable to pay their bill in the past six months: *"I've been laid off." "I'm doing the best I can."*

The bottom line is that you will never please a debt collector. They are after the money. So they hope to stress you out beyond belief until you send them your child's lunch money!

You don't have to listen to the name-calling and angry voices screaming at you. Just hang up! And try using the phone features listed in *Strategy #4* before you answer your phone next time.

Strategy #2
Can You Hear
Me Now?

Many times debt collectors place your number on a robocall, causing your home telephone to ring several times a day.

You have already told them several times that your current financial situation prevents you from being able to pay at the moment, but of course they won't listen.

One solution may be to disconnect your home telephone and strictly use a cell phone. This will totally prevent calls at home from pesky debt collectors. Plus, cell phone numbers are private and are not listed in a telephone directory (well, not yet anyway). Moreover, with the right calling plan and smart usage, cell phones can be more affordable than home phones.

Strategy #3
"The Number You Have Reached"

fast way to stop debt collector calls is to simply change your home telephone number. The telephone company charges a fee for this service; however, in cases where you are being harassed, they will sometimes change it for free.

After your number is changed, the telephone company provides a special recording for those who call the old number that will either give the caller your new number or state that your number has been changed to an unpublished number.

You should waive both these options. Instead, inform the telephone company that you want a recording that states your number is no longer in service. A debt collector hearing this recording will assume that your phone was disconnected for non-payment and stop calling.

Strategy #4
Use the Phone

Many of us know to use call screening features provided by our telephone company as a way to avoid harassing debt collector calls. However, many people don't use any feature other than their Caller ID as a call screen method. Caller ID allows you to see the identity of an incoming call while you are on or off the telephone before you answer the call. This is a no-brainer. You only answer calls from numbers you recognize. Hence, you avoid debt collectors. Many other telephone features can be used more cleverly. Here are the best features:

Multi-Ring or Distinctive Ring allows you to obtain additional telephone numbers that ring on the same line; each number has a different ring. Use one number for friends and family and the other for your debt collectors. Just keep straight which ring goes with the appropriate party.

Voicemail vs. Answering Machine: As you know, voicemail accepts messages while you are away from home or currently on a call. I like voicemail because it is private; other people (like friends and neighbors) cannot hear the messages while they are being left. You wouldn't want your visitors overhearing a message being left on your answering machine from an angry debt collector demanding payment. You'll be the gossip topic for weeks to come: "Hey, guess who isn't paying their bills?"

Call Screening allows you to create a "do not accept" list of telephone numbers. Callers from the numbers on the list will hear a message indicating that their call will not be accepted. You could use this feature to create a list of harassing debt collector phone numbers and prevent their calls from getting through.

Privacy Manager prevents incoming calls from anonymous callers. This feature is a debt collector's nightmare because they have to show a number to get through. Now you have a number to add to your "do not accept" list.

Although these call screen features on your telephone may work for minor debts, they only bandage those major debt collection issues such as a past-due car note. In other words, this strategy will not prevent you from walking out of the grocery store and discovering that your car has been repossessed. We will discuss ways to avoid vehicle repossession in Strategy #10.

Strategy #5
Lie Like A Rug!

et's just assume that you live on Mars and do not have any of the phone features listed in *Strategy #4* or for some unknown reason you get caught on the phone with a debt collector. What do you do? Here are a few suggestions: Tell them they have the wrong number. Tell them that you don't live there anymore. Tell them you skipped town and *you* are looking for *yourself* also. Tell them you are in a self-induced coma. Heck, use your imagination. Here's an example of what such a conversation might sound like:

> **Debt collector:** May I speak with Lisa Doe?

Lisa: Sorry, you have the wrong number.

Debt Collector: Is this 555-5555?

Lisa: No, it is 555-5556.

Debt Collector: Sorry.

Lisa: That's okay.

(She doesn't answer the phone when the debt collector calls right back.)

Here is another example:

Debt Collector: May I speak with James Doe?

James Doe: He's not here.

Debt Collector: I am calling about a credit card bill that is ninety days past due (debt collectors *will* tell your business).

James Doe: Well, I don't mind letting you know that lowdown James was my roommate. He skipped town, owing me over a grand in rent and utilities. I'm looking for him, too.

Debt Collector: What a shame. People like that are a disgrace.

James: Yeah, I can think of a better word than that. (*Both laugh.*)

Debt Collector: Well, if you catch up with him, tell him to call 1-800-555-...

James: I'll do you one better. I'll call you *myself* and give you any new information I find out about that snake in the grass.

Debt Collector: Thanks, buddy.

James: No prob.

Why lie? Well, it is totally an individual decision, of course, but here are three good reasons: (1) You don't have the money; (2) You just don't have the money; and (the third one is my favorite) (3) You really, honestly just don't have the money!

Telling most debt collectors that you don't have the money to pay them—even though it is the truth—is the same as saying "Blah, Blah, Blah!"

Strategy #6
I Cannot Tell A Lie!

I f you are just beginning your downhill spiral into debt, being truthful by explaining to your creditors that you have just lost your job or that your spouse is terminally ill just might grant you a bit of amnesty, especially if you were a steadfast, well-paying customer in the past.

Creditors have been known to grant a little leeway early on by allowing you to pay them what you can for a while or just paying on the interest. Well, if all you need is a little leeway, then this might very well be the way to go. However, if you are up to your eyeballs in debt and can't see your way clear in the very near future, that compassionate customer service rep "Nice Nancy" will grow impatient and quickly turn you over to "Sherman the Shark" in their collections department.

But you're not scared. You consider yourself a pretty patient and straightforward person who is not easily rattled. Plus, you do not mind talking to Tom, Linda, or Jeff or whatever your debt collector is calling himself or herself. As a matter of fact, you enjoy a good stressful telephone conversation every now and again. Well, Honest Jack, look forward to a conversation similar to this one:

Collections: May I speak with Jack?

Honest Jack: Speaking.

Collections: Jack, this is Jeff from XYZ Collection Agency and I am calling about your account that is six months past due.

Honest Jack: Yeah, I know, but like I told you guys yesterday, I have been out of work for six months and I am a little short on cash.

Collections: Well, can't you send us something?

Honest Jack: Nope. Sorry, Jeff. I just can't do it.

Collections: Six months is a long time to be sitting around the house out of work, Jack!

Honest Jack: Tell me about it!

Collections: Are you looking?

Honest Jack: Yep, looking every day. No luck.

Collections: Well, can't you borrow the money from a family member?

Honest Jack: No, but could you loan me the money?

Collections: Hey, I didn't get you into this mess!

Honest Jack: Neither did my family members.

Collections: Well, they love you. I don't!

Honest Jack: (chuckles) You don't know my family members, Jeff.

Collections: Well, my seventeen-year-old son got a job at Mickey D's his first day out looking for work!

Honest Jack: Think he'll loan me the money?

Collections: You're getting a big kick out of this, aren't you?

Honest Jack: Not really. You're not as fun as the last guy.

Collections: Look! You were extended a line of credit in good faith!

Honest Jack: No, I was extended a line of credit because I made $60,000 a year and was able to pay my bills on time. Unfortunately, I don't make that kind of money anymore—wish I did. But as soon as I get back on my feet, I will plan to pay my debts.

Collections: Well, you're eating and your telephone is on so you must have *some* money!

28

Honest Jack: Thanks to unemployment, I am able to feed my family and keep my telephone on in case of an emergency or if someone calls about a job. But there is not much left over to pay my bills.

Collections: I suggest that you take a job flipping burgers because I am not going to go away! Send us at least a hundred dollars by the close of business tomorrow or else—!

Honest Jack: I know, I know. You are going to take more drastic steps.

Collections: Look, you loser! It's people like you that give good credit a bad name!

Honest Jack: Ah, gotta go, Jeff. I told you guys the rules: no name-calling. Bye. Have a good day! *(Hangs up on the debt collector screaming obscenities.)*

Most of us are not as patient as Jack and wouldn't want to put up with a call like that one. By

the way, that example was from a *decent* debt collector. They get much worse than that!

Strategy #7
The Bad Credit
Welcome Wagon

You have managed to evade those heartless debt collectors for months while you get your finances in order. However, this process has left you with a low credit rating. You see an ad for Slick Fred's Bargain Furniture with the caption, "Bad Credit Welcomed. Everyone is approved." Your sofa is coming apart, so you rush in to apply for the credit needed to buy the furniture.

Slick Fred bursts your bubble when he gives you a quick lesson on what his rendition of what *approved* really means: (1) you are approved only with a co-signer; (2) you are approved at ridiculously high interest rates; (3) you are approved for an amount so low that you need an incredibly high down payment to get the furniture.

Unfortunately, at this point, it does not matter whether you walk away with the cheap, overpriced furniture or not. This is the least of your worries because the damage has already been done. You've awakened the proverbial sleeping credit giant!

Once your credit was checked, all of your current information was given to the credit bureau, and the debt collectors who constantly look for updates in your credit file have a fresh new lead on you. Your peace and quiet is over. Debt collectors are calling and writing again while you sit mumbling regrets to yourself on that cheap, overpriced sofa!

Remember, the plan is to pull yourself together first. Forget about new credit until you are able to rebuild your finances. This may include finishing school, starting a new business, or working back up the corporate ladder. Once you have gotten back on track and paid off those old debts, you can legitimately apply for credit to buy quality furniture. In the meantime, buy a roll of duct tape to repair that broken sofa you currently own.

Beware of claims to repair or erase bad credit — for a fee, of course. After you complete all the paperwork and hear the mumbo jumbo, the self-proclaimed "credit repairer" walks away with your money, leaving your poor credit rating intact.

Bad credit does not disappear overnight. It involves three simple steps: 1) paying down debt, 2) paying on time, and 3) using credit responsibly. There are no other ways around it. If you're going through hard times, following those steps may be difficult at the moment. But once your financial condition improves, you can repair your credit all by yourself — free of charge!

Instant loan approval is another common rip-off used against people going through hard times. You'll get one of those check replicas in the mail written out in your name for, let's say, $7,500, along with that infamous phrase, *Bad Credit Welcome!*

All you need to do is call the number attached to the phony check for instant loan approval. Once you call, they tell you that your low credit rating doesn't matter and the loan program is designed to help you rebuild your credit. You just pay them a few hundred dollars *"up front"* to cover *"loan processing and other fees"* or *"make the first payment in advance,"* and the money is yours! Yeah, right! It's more like, your money is theirs because once you pay their "fees," no check ever materializes and you are left duped out of money you couldn't afford to lose in the first place.

This scam is not only used for bogus loans; it can also take the form of some type of "grand prize" they say you have won. In order to claim your prize, you must pay some outlandish shipping and handling costs (there goes those fees again). If you are approached with this offer and your common sense doesn't kick in, a little research with the Better Business Bureau can save you a lot of headache.

A simple rule: if it sounds too good to be true, then it probably is!

Strategy #8
They Think You're Stupid?

nfortunately, when you are going through hard times, people try to take advantage of you. Strategy #7 is just one example. Many businesses believe that because people have less than perfect credit, they can not only charge them ridiculously high interest rates for ridiculously shoddy merchandise, but also lure them into utilizing certain loan and rental services designed for people who are in a financial rut such as title loans, payday loans. and rent-to-own furniture stores.

Title loan establishments allow you to use the title to your automobile as collateral to get a loan without a credit check. If you are in a position to pay back this loan right away (less than a month), it might be considered a good strategy. However, that is normally NOT the case. If this were the case, the title loan business would be out of business.

I bet when Mr. Title Loan came up with the idea for this business, he knew the people he planned to target as customers would be down on their luck and desperate. Mr. Title Loan also knew that though his customers hoped to pay off the loan quickly, their circumstances would force them into long, drawn-out monthly payments that would equal mega bucks for the title loan business.

One lady found this out firsthand when she borrowed $2,000 against her automobile that had a Blue Book value of more than $6,000. She'd hoped to be able to settle the loan in a couple of months, but one financial crisis led to another, and then another. In the end, it took her eighteen months to finally pay off the title loan—to the tune of $3,600 in interest! (10 percent per month for 18 months or $200 a month x 18

=$3,600). Sounds like a legalized form of loan shark-ing!

Payday loan outfits are no better. These types of loans are tempting. They easily lure in customers because they are quick, short-term, and usually do not lend more than $1,500. The core of the payday loan's survival is their ability to attract people who are in financial strains and need quick cash.

The payday loan scheme works like this: Let's say you need $450. You write four postdated checks to the payday loan store totaling the amount you need, plus about $70 in finance charges, for a total of $520. You get the postdated checks back once you pay them in full.

In addition, you sign a wage assignment document effective the date of the loan in order to speed things along in case you don't pay or those postdated checks you gave them bounce.

Although $70 is terribly high interest on such a small loan, people who have an emergency situation agree to it. When the loan period is up (usually two weeks), you can either hand over the $520 in cash and get your personal checks back OR continue to pay $70 every two weeks for nine payments, with a final balloon payment of $520.

That $70 you paid every two weeks was not paying down the loan. It was just finance charges for taking out the loan. You would need to pay an amount *more than* $70 to make a dent in the principal! So, if you cannot pay off your loan early (they are hoping you can't), you could end up paying $1,150 on a $450 loan! ($70 x 9= $630 + $520 = $1,150).

These businesses are enticing because the charges seem lower than the fees you could rack up in bank services charges for nonsufficient funds transactions. Most banks charge upwards of $35 for each transaction. For example, if you do not have the funds in your bank account to cover five checks or debits totaling $60, it could cost you $175 in fees at most banks. On top of that, you are charged a daily overdraft fee of about $5.00.

That's a lot of money when compared to the $70 interest from a payday loan store, but at least the bank reaches a limit and closes your account, if necessary. They don't let it drag on for months in the hopes of collecting additional fees; plus, with proper management of your account, checking account NSF fees can be avoided.

Finally, be leery of rent-to-own furniture stores that offer long contracts with low weekly payments. Most people are lured in by the low weekly charges. For instance, a brand name computer would cost you around $25 per week, but at the end of a two-year contract, you end up paying $2,600! The computer retails at $599, which means you paid more than four times the retail price for that computer! You were better off saving $25 a week for six months and buying the computer outright.

When you are going through hard times, try not to allow a desperate situation to cause you to be taken advantage of. You might be broke, but you're not stupid.

Strategy #9
Shut Up!

I f you get a new job, don't share the information with your soon-to-be previous employer, especially if debt collector calls at work have been a problem for you. Although previous employers are not supposed to reveal personal information about you, vicious debt collectors use clever methods to get needed information.

Remember Spiteful Susie? You know, the secretary who never liked you much anyway. Well, she would love to stick it to you by telling a debt collector anything they want to know about you from your personnel file.

Don't forget about Helpful Helen, the ultra-nice receptionist who could willingly provide information to a "relative" of yours who simply wants to inform you of a dying grandmother. Helpful Helen is so naïve that she does not realize she is actually speaking to a debt collector who is posing as a relative to get updated information on you.

The debt collectors can also get new information about where you are employed from the information you provide on a new credit application or updates you make to existing creditors, such as a change of address. Give yourself a break. Keep your mouth shut!

Strategy #10
Hide That Car?

ehicle repossession may appear justified in certain circumstances where a person is generally being irresponsible and otherwise able to meet their financial obligation, but chooses not to. But what about that hardworking person who paid their monthly automobile payment dutifully for years? Then, suddenly, they fall into hard times and missed a couple of payments. Why should their car be repossessed? Shouldn't they get some type of reprieve for paying on time for so many years?

Basically, the lender owns your car until it is <u>paid in full</u>. Therefore, even one missed payment could be considered a breach of your contract. It gets worse. After they repo your car, they can sue you for what is called deficiency. Deficiency is any amount still owed on your contract AFTER your lender sells your repossessed vehicle at—let's say—an auction. Often they sell your car for less than they expected you to pay to get it back! What do they care if they are going to sue you for the difference anyway?

Imagine paying $18,000 in payments on your vehicle over time with $5,000 left before the car is paid in full. Suddenly, without warning, you lose your job and fall behind a couple of months with the payments. The next thing you know, your vehicle gets repossessed.

Now you must pay triple the amount of the two months you were delinquent because of added repossession and storage costs. You cannot come up with the money, because if you had the money, your vehicle would not have been repossessed in the first place! Eventually, your car is sold at an auction for $3,500. You are then sued for the remaining balance of $1,500 you owed on the vehicle, plus the repo costs!

Okay, what is the point of this? If they are going to sue you for the unpaid balance anyway, why not just give you the opportunity to pay the bill? Wouldn't they come out better in the long run? Duh!

Bottom line: The repo man doesn't care that your finances are in limbo because you have recently divorced or that your employer informed you in the eleventh hour that you were being laid off. The repo man only cares about the fees that they will collect once they recover your vehicle for the lender.

There is no negotiating with the repo man, so once they hook your car up to their truck, there is no stopping them. Your only hope is to avoid them. Not by hiding your car, but buying some time. Here are five options to consider:

1. **Communicate!** Call the lender before they call you. Relentlessly stay in contact with the lender to explain your situation. Provide updates on how your job search is coming. Write letters to the president of the finance company or bank, detailing your solid payment history in the past, outlining how you ended

up in your current situation, and explaining why you need your vehicle. It's a long shot, but maybe someone out there may have a heart.

Try to pay what you can to show good faith. Try anything that will separate you from the pack and demonstrate that you are a human being and not just an account number. Every finance company has a collection timeline they follow. Of course, the longer your payments are late, the more aggressive their collections efforts become.

2. Depending on how long you have owned your vehicle, the quality of the vehicle, and the number of payments you have left, you may want **to sell it privately and pay off the loan**. This only works if you owe less on your vehicle than it is worth. For example, let's say you can easily sell your vehicle for $6,000 and you owe $4,000. You could sell it, pay off the loan and have $2,000 toward buying another vehicle.

3. To bring your payments down, you could try to **refinance at a lower interest rate or spread payments over a longer period of time**. The down-

side is the amount of interest you pay in the long run would increase, but you would avoid repo costs and have a more affordable payment. If your credit is still decent, this may be an option that the finance company would extend to you.

4. You could also attempt to **trade in your vehicle for a more affordable one**. If you have less than perfect credit, your new interest rate could be higher, but your monthly note would be less. Before considering the trade, find out what the resale value is on your car compared to how much you owe. If there is not much resale value in the automobile you are trading or you owe a lot on it, the remaining balance will be tacked onto the new car and your payments could be worse.

5. **Find someone to take over your car payments**. Contact your lender to see whether they will rewrite your loan in the name of the other person. If that doesn't work, you can consider writing an agreement between you and the person willing to take over your car payments. This option is pretty

47

risky because the car will still be in your name. Plus, you'll have to ask yourself, *"Will this person just make matters worse?"* After all, if they have good credit, why do they need to take over your payments? Couldn't they just buy their own car? So, if you decide to take this route, make sure you find an attorney to help you draw up a legally binding agreement.

The reality is that finance companies and banks are in business to make money — it's all about the Benjamins. Therefore, delinquent payments will not be tolerated until the cows come home. But with the right initiative, good communication, and a lot of luck, rules can be bent, stretched, and broken in your favor. What do you have to lose?

I heard about a guy who switched cars with his brother who lived in a different state. Within six months, he straightens out his finances and paid his six-month delinquent car note to date, plus late fees. He saved himself the high cost of repossession and storage fees, deficiency costs, and the embarrassment of having his car repossessed (neighbors do watch).

Good for him, but I would be leery of taking such a chance. Depending on how much is owed on your vehicle and its resale value, the lender may find it worth their while to take you to court to recover the vehicle.

Built-in tracking devices are becoming more prevalent on newer vehicles as an anti-theft deterrent. However, your lender won't think twice to use that device installed for your protection against you.

Therefore, if you have a tracking device on your car, the amount of time you can hide your vehicle is greatly decreased depending upon how aggressively your lender wants your car. Your lender just might send the repo man to retrieve your car you've hidden at your uncle's house 500 miles away in Texas and ship it back at your expense!

Strategy #11
Take My Car...Please!

ood News: You quickly find a job after being laid off for a couple of months. Bad News: Your new job pays $25,000 less a year. You obviously need to shave your budget and soon realize that your luxury car has to go.

The options discussed in *"Hide That Car"* will not work because it is not just a matter of catching up on car payments—you can no longer afford the car. On top of that, you owe too much on your car to trade it in or sell it. And the risk of finding someone to take over your car note doesn't appeal to you. So, what can you do besides wait for the repo man to show up at your door? One option is to have your car voluntarily repossessed.

Voluntary repossession basically means that you call the finance company and tell them you can no longer afford the payments and want them to take it back. They will either come get the vehicle or tell you where to drop it off.

By getting rid of the car you couldn't afford and would eventually lose to the repo man anyway, you now have one less thing to worry about while you are going through hard times. And it gives your lender an opportunity to sell the car to someone else.

This option is extreme, but it is better than having your vehicle repossessed while you're singing in the church choir on Sunday morning or attending a parent-teacher conference!

Bear in mind that a vehicle repossession will likely show on your credit report. The fact that you volunteered to give the car back doesn't change that.

Strategy #12
Sue Their Pants Off!

ccording to the Fair Debt Collection Practices Act (FDCPA), Section 813, an individual can sue a debt collector for as much as $1,000 and a group of people can file a class action suit and recover as much as $500,000 or 1 percent of the net worth of the debt collector.

The Fair Debt Collection Practices Act, which is enforced by the Federal Trade Commission (FTC), takes violations of the FDCPA very seriously. A debt buyer/debt collection business called CAMCO, RM Financial was ordered to pay a $300,000 civil penalty for violation of the Fair Debt Collection Practices Act:

CAMCO is a debt buyer. A company that buys old debts well past the statute of limitations and attempts to collect them. Most of the debts are unenforceable in court and are also so old that they are beyond the reporting periods allowed under the Fair Credit Reporting Act. Some of the debts CAMCO allegedly attempted to collect were already discharged in bankruptcy or had been paid. The FTC charged that in their attempt to collect these debts, the companies engaged in abusive and deceptive collection practices, including:

- *Harassing consumers at their workplaces;*
- *Discussing consumers' debts with third parties;*
- *Continuing to communicate with consumers after consumers had notified them that they did not owe the money and did not wish to be contacted again;*
- *Using obscene or profane language;*

- *Calling consumers continuously with the intention of annoying and abusing them;*
- *Falsely representing the amount and legal status of the debts;*
- *Misrepresenting themselves as attorneys;*
- *Threatening imprisonment, seizure, garnishment, attachment or sale of property or wages with full knowledge that such action could not legally be taken;*
- *Threatening to take action that could not be legally taken, including threatening to disclose the debts to consumers' employers and threatening to report the debt to consumer reporting agencies even though the debts are past the credit reporting periods; and*
- *Ignoring consumer's disputes of the charges and continuing to harass them*

after consumers requested verification
of the debts.

Unfortunately, thousands of people are experiencing this type of harassment every day.

If you decide to file suit, it is not an easy task. In order to win a battle against the debt collectors, you must have proof. So, become familiar with the Fair Debt Collection Practices Act so you will know right away what laws the debt collector is violating. Keep a journal. Record the harassing conversations and telephone messages and contact your attorney general's office with your evidence.

Hopefully, you'll win enough to pay off your debt, courtesy of the debt collector!

Strategy #13
Know Your Rights

T he Fair Debt Collection Act outlines several laws to protect the consumer against abusive debt collectors. Here are some of the good ones to know:

Section 806(2): The use of obscene or profane language the natural consequence of which is to abuse the hearer or reader. *[Translation: Debt collectors cannot use offensive language or call you bad names like "loser" or "deadbeat."]*

Section 806(5): Causing a telephone to ring or engaging any person in telephone conversation repeatedly or continuously with intent to annoy, abuse, or harass any person at the called number. *[Transla-*

tion: Debt collectors cannot call you over and over again to get on your nerves.]

Section 807(5): The threat to take any action that cannot legally be taken or that is not intended to be taken. *[Translation: Debt collectors cannot threaten to have you arrested for not paying your debt.]*

Section 807(10): The use of any false representation or deceptive means to collect or attempt to collect any debt or to obtain information concerning a consumer.

[Translation: Debt collectors can't pretend to be someone they are not, like a relative or an attorney.]

Section 812(a): It is unlawful to design, compile, and furnish any form knowing that such form would be used to create the false belief in a consumer that a person other than the creditor of such consumer is participating in the collection of or in an attempt to collect a debt such consumer allegedly owes such creditor, when in fact such person is not so participating. *[Translation: For example, debt collectors cannot send* *a postcard saying you have won a free cruise to get you to call them.]*

As you can see, many debt collectors violate the Fair Debt Collection Practices Act frequently. I suggest that you educate yourself and read the FDCPA in its entirety.

Debt collectors are counting on you not being familiar with the law because if you do not know what the laws are, you cannot fight against them. It will knock a debt collector off his feet to hear you say, "You are violating Section 806 Paragraph 2 of the Fair Debt Collection Practices Act and I am going to report you!"

Strategy #14
The Power Of The Pen

When dealing with debt collectors, you have more power than you think. Most people believe that debt collectors can call you whether you like it or not. This is not true. According to the Fair Debt Collection Practices Act Section 805, you can write a letter to a debt collector requesting that they *"cease further communication"* with you. At the moment they receive your letter, "the debt collector shall not communicate further" with you.

Make sure this letter is sent certified mail with a signature request receipt. If they continue to call, you may use your return receipt from the post office as evidence in the event you decide to Sue Their Pants Off! (Strategy #12).

There are a few exceptions where the debt collector can contact you after they have received your letter, but only to: (1) inform you that they will discontinue collection efforts; (2) inform you of any special remedies (legal action) they will invoke; or (3) to invoke special remedies.

Strategy #15
Tricks Of The Trade

We have discussed several tactics throughout this book that debt collectors use to find you.. Those of you who have been broke for a while know about these tricks of the trade, but you newbies may not. Here are a few to be aware of:

• You get a postcard for a free oil change at your local auto dealership. The catch is that the free service is only available on a certain day during a short two-hour time span. When you arrive and hand over your keys, the repo man drives away.

• Someone shows up to your home wearing a phony badge, claiming to be from the sheriff's department and demanding the keys and/or the location of your automobile. Frightened that you will be arrested, you hand over the keys or divulge the whereabouts of the vehicle. And the repo man drives away into the sunset.

• Debt collectors get their hands on your telephone records and call the numbers you frequently call to get information or leave "urgent" messages. Car repossession services are notorious for this. They will call your friends and family, pretending to be investigator so-and-so or detective whoever in an attempt to find out where your automobile is.

• You get a letter in the mail that reads: "We have been trying to reach you to inform you that you are the guaranteed winner of a brand new car. Call 888-888-8888 to claim your prize." You excitedly call the number and answer a series of questions for "verification purposes," including your home address, where you work, your daytime phone number, and the phone number of a close relative. After all the information is collected, your mouth falls to the floor when you discover you are actually speaking to a debt collector! Now, instead of being the winner of a new car, you are the proud winner of the Fool of the Year Award. The grand prize: Wage Garnishment!

Strategy #16
Make Them Prove It!

O ften there are third-party debt collectors who are not acting on behalf of the creditor you owe. Instead, they go after old debt that your creditors wrote off years ago. Although your debt was written off, your original creditor still sells it for a fraction of what you owe. For example, your original creditor can sell your $500 credit card debt to a third-party collection agency for $50. The third-party debt collector then tries to collect the original $500 from you, plus interest. If they can get you to pay even $125, they have profited big-time.

They do this by posing as litigation firms out to sue you for the entire amount, plus interest. Their paperwork looks legal and they sound very stern and menacing on the telephone. Don't let them scare you. Put the burden back in their laps and make them prove that they are acting on behalf of your original creditor and have the legal right to pursue you.

Millions of people are in debt. This equates to millions of pieces of paperwork. Often this paperwork gets lost in the shuffle, misplaced, or destroyed. This can work in your favor. Ask for the original paperwork showing your signature. Ask for the breakdown of what you owe, including interest. Many third-party debt collectors do not have this information, which weakens their ability to legally collect from you. If they can't prove it, you don't have to pay it.

Strategy #17
Save Your House

So many good people lose their homes without knowing what options are available to them. Consider these alternatives to save your home:

Special forbearance: Your lender may be able to arrange a repayment plan based on your financial situation. Your lender may even provide for a temporary reduction or suspension of your payments. You may qualify for this if you have recently lost your job or your source of income, or if you had an unexpected increase in living expenses. You must furnish information to your lender to show that you would be able to meet the requirements of the new payment plan.

Mortgage modification: You may be able to re-finance the debt and/or extend the term of your mortgage loan. This may help you catch up by reducing the monthly payments to a more affordable level. You may qualify if you have recovered from a financial problem but your net income is less than it was before the default (failure to pay).

Partial claim: Your lender may be able to work with you to obtain an interest-free loan from US Department of Housing and Urban Development (HUD) to bring your mortgage current. You may qualify if: 1) your loan is at least four months delinquent but no more than twelve months delinquent; 2) your mortgage is not in foreclosure; and 3) you are able to begin making full mortgage payments. When your lender files a partial claim, HUD will pay your lender the amount necessary to bring your mortgage current. You must execute a promissory note, and a lien will be placed on your property until the promissory note is paid in full. The promissory note is interest-free and will be due if you sell or leave your property, or when your mortgage matures.

Pre-foreclosure sale (Short Sale): This will allow you to sell your property and pay off your mortgage loan to avoid foreclosure and damage to your credit rating. You may qualify if: 1) the "as is" appraised value is at least 70 percent of the amount you owe and the sales price is 95 percent of the appraised value; 2) the loan is at least two months delinquent prior to the pre-foreclosure sale closing date; and 3) you are able to sell your house within three to five months (depending on what your lender agrees to). An additional benefit to this option is the assistance you will receive with the seller-paid closing costs.

Deed-in-lieu of foreclosure: As a last resort, you may be able to voluntarily "give back" your property to the lender. This won't save your house, but it will help your chances of getting another mortgage loan in the future. You can qualify if: 1) you are in default and don't qualify for any of the other options; 2) your attempts at selling the house before foreclosure were unsuccessful; and 3) you don't have another FHA mortgage in default.

Since this book was initially published in 2005, the housing crisis hit. As a result, many new programs were developed to help homeowners save their homes. One of the best ones is the Making Home Affordable Program. The MHAP is designed to help homeowners' lower mortgage payments to an affordable rate with as little as two percent interest. The deadline for this program has been extended to December 31, 2015.

Strategy #18
First Things First

Always pay priority bills first, especially when you are short on cash. The top three priorities are: (1) Rent/Mortgage; (2) Car Payment; and (3) Utilities. All creditors are worthy to be paid and you should not ignore the fact that you owe them money. However, when hard times set in, you have to make hard choices.

Don't let a debt collector harass you into paying a $200 delinquent cable bill, only to end up lighting candles because you could not pay the electric bill! Instead, sacrifice the cable, tell them what you are going through and that you intend to pay them the minute your situation improves.

It may seem like an odd move to place your car payment before utility payments. But without a car to get to work or find work, you could risk losing your job or having difficulty finding one. You may be able to find assistance with your utilities from various social service agencies (*see Strategy #34*). But there are no social service agencies that will help you pay your car note! Plus, you can always cut back on utility usage to save money. And it is easier to get your utilities reconnected than it is to get your car back from the repo man!

Perhaps your home and work are accessible to public transportation, and you don't own a car. In that case, move the cost of your monthly bus or train fare to the number two slot, but *always* pay your rent or mortgage first! Keeping a roof over your head should be the top priority, especially if you have children.

Strategy #19
Rob Peter To Pay Paul

P eople who have been truly broke already know all too well the expression "Robbing Peter to Pay Paul." The term has been around for centuries. It basically means using money set aside for one debt to pay another. For instance, money allotted to pay credit card bills may have to be used to help pay the rent or mortgage, which is a greater priority as stated in the previous strategy. Therefore, you are metaphorically robbing the money set allotted to pay the credit card bills to satisfy the mortgage/rent bill. When faced with the possibility of eviction, this option may stop the local sheriff from throwing your belongings "to the curb."

Another Robbing Peter to Pay Paul scenario involves incurring more debt to satisfy another debt. For example, taking a cash advance from a credit card to pay the rent or using a credit card to pay the utility bill. This is usually the step taken by a person who is suddenly thrown in the jaws of broke-ness due to loss of job, loss of income due to illness, etc. and is trying to save their credit rating.

Unfortunately, the typical broke man does not have the funds to commit either options of debt robbery because they are just trying to survive with the little income they have at their disposal.

Strategy #20
Your Name Please?

Your name becomes important when you need to have your utilities or telephone connected. Many people decide to use their mother's, brother's, sister's, and even their children's name to have various utilities reconnected after their services were disconnected for non-payment. Using false names is definitely the wrong way to go. Not only because it is an act of fraud against the utility companies, but also because there is a better solution.

Fortunately, there are various programs and payment plans available through utility companies to help you meet your obligations. Here are four to consider before you use your Grandpa Joe's name:

74

1. Set up a budget billing plan. This plan gives you a specific amount to pay each month for a year at a time. When you are going through hard times, it helps to know exactly what you owe instead of crossing your fingers every month, hoping the amount you owe is not more than you can afford.

2. Deferred billing plans are also available. This allows you to pay off your delinquent amount over a specified period of time (usually up to twelve months) while making your current monthly payments.

3. Special programs have been developed for people with serious illnesses. If you qualify, this method provides leniency against disconnection. Some utility companies require doctor's verification on file as proof of the illness before your account is granted this special status, which must be updated each month.

4. Many of your local social service agencies provide utility assistance when you have a disconnection notice.

Consider the above four options if you are having trouble paying utilities. That way, when the utility company customer service rep asks you your name, you won't break into a cold sweat from the stress of trying to keep track of all the aliases you've used in the past!

Strategy #21
Temporary Hardship

S ome credit card companies and banks offer hardship programs to help customers who are having financial difficulties. Although hardship programs benefits vary, they usually reduce your minimum payment, eliminate late fees, and lower your interest rate for 6 months to a year.

These programs are not advertised so you will have to contact your credit card company directly. Call the customer service department and explain your hardship (i.e. lay off, illness, increase in expenses, decrease in income) and they will transfer you the right department. No need to submit a hardship letter or sign any special agreement. The terms will be discussed with you over the phone and a letter will be mailed to you confirming your participation.

Don't worry about not qualifying for the program. If you are enduring financial hardships, you will most likely be eligible. The only thing that may prevent you from qualifying would be if your payments are current. Although you may have just been laid off and anticipate financial difficulties, some credit card companies need to see a late payment history.

Your account will be suspended from future purchases until you complete the program, but this shouldn't be a problem since you should not be increasing your debt anyway. Some credit card companies report your participation in the hardship program to the credit bureau so if that is a concern, you should ask. Either way it will be removed from the credit bureau once you have completed the program.

Finally, be sure to make the payments on time. If you miss a payment or two, the hardship agreement will be cancelled, your interest rate will go back

up and you will be expected to make regular payments. Therefore, be sure to accept a payment plan
that you can afford.

Strategy #22
That Good Faith Effort

D epending on how broke you are, you may be able to pay *something* to your creditors, even if it is below the minimum amount due. Something is better than nothing, especially if you are doing your best.

Paying even $10 a month on a $25 monthly payment shows a good faith effort. Even if the creditors do not appreciate it (they will still charge you a late fee), it gets you in the habit of remembering your obligation and honoring it the best you can. When you can pay more, do so. A little bit goes a long way and your debt will chip away over time. Later on down the line, when you are negotiating the debt payoff, your good faith effort will be considered and may even prevent your account from being sold to the piranhas.

Strategy #23
Pay Them

===

Hurray! You have survived. You have gotten back on your feet. You have a good job that pays well. Or maybe you started a small business that is profitable. The cash is rolling in again. Now it is time to pay back your creditors. When you were broke and trying to survive, you couldn't pay them. You had to focus on keeping a roof over your head and food on the table for your family. That is understandable, but now that you are no longer broke, it is time to live up to your obligations.

You might be asking why you should pay them. After all these years, they have probably written off your debt anyway. You've weathered the storm. It's time to ride off into the sunset.

Consider it this way. Think of a loan that you gave someone years ago who promised to pay you back, but never did. Perhaps it severed a long friend- ship or family relationship. If they finally come back to you years later with the money, wouldn't you be grateful? Well, do unto others as you would have them do unto you.

Call your original creditors one by one and work out a repayment schedule. Often you can nego- tiate what you owe them by shaving off the penalty and interest. Even if you have not paid them in years, they more than likely still have your record on file. Sometimes the original creditor cannot accept the payment from you due to the agreement with the third-party debt collector that purchased your debt. In this case, they may refer you to them and you are forced to negotiate with the devil.

Section II
Surviving Life's
Little Setbacks

W e have covered strategies to survive the hazards of debt collectors, debt traps, and juggling bills. Now we will focus on how to keep food on the table, a roof over your head, and keep your sanity in the meantime.

Life is full of bumps in the road, obstacles, and unforeseen circumstances. Maybe the company where you worked for twenty years decided to lay you off so that they could outsource jobs to a foreign company or decided to use temp workers to save a few bucks. Perhaps a routine visit to the doctor turned into a diagnosed illness that caused you to miss work for more than a year.

Strategies 24-50 will show you some ways to live through and emerge from the pitfalls of living the broke life and hopefully help you make sure these temporary setbacks in life do not become a permanent way of life.

Strategy #24
Do The Hustle

===================

You cannot always depend on others to employ you or pay you enough money to make ends meet, but you can always depend on yourself. People have been working side hustles for years. Remember Grandma selling her homemade pear preserves, garden vegetables, and quilts? That was her hustle. If we think hard enough, all of us can figure out legitimate ways to earn extra cash.

In most cases, you can turn something that you do well into extra cash. For example, if you are a singer, you could contract out to sing at weddings, funerals, or special events. If you repair automobiles, paint houses, bake scrumptious cookies, or fix small appliances—then repair, paint, bake, fix and charge a fee for your services. If you are able to sew or design craft items—then sew, design and *charge*. If you are a trained dancer, teach dance and *charge*. If you are well versed in computer operation or repair, give lessons, repair and—you guessed it—*charge!* You get the point. The list of options is endless.

If you do not feel you have any marketable skills, you can always learn. One woman taught herself how to design personalized gift baskets for special occasions to earn extra income. She got so good at it that she was hired to teach the craft at a local community college.

Another man turned what his wife referred to as junk around the house into $3,000 in eBay sales. When he ran out of items, he began to rummage around garage sales and flea markets for bargains that earned huge profits online.

If you are unsure about what you can do, there are many books with tons of ideas about ways to earn extra income (you can check them out for free at your local library). Once you decide what you want to do, get the word out by posting flyers everywhere (*do not forget those social networks*) and watch what happens! You might drum up enough business to turn your side hustle into a lucrative small business.

Strategy #25
Part-Timers

The ominous condition of the labor force makes it difficult to find suitable full-time employment. If you are fortunate enough to land an entry-level position, expect to work long hours for a low salary. Of course, if you are a recent college grad still living with your parents, you can afford to live off your $20,000 a year entry-level position for a few years while you pay your dues. However, if you have a family to support with a mortgage and other household bills, then that entry-level income won't go very far.

Consider working multiple part-time jobs to make ends meet. Many actors and musicians survive part-timing it and are sometimes able to pull in up-wards of $50,000 a year or more with this method.

Having multiple jobs also helps to enhance your resume with the diverse skill sets you obtained from working in different jobs. Some people prefer having multiple part-time jobs because it prevents them from getting bored by the mundane tasks of a forty-hour workweek.

Part-time work doesn't always have to be per-formed at brick and mortar establishments such as department stores or the local coffee shop. A lot of part-time work can be done sitting behind your com-puter performing duties such as working as a virtual assistant or a freelance web designer. Many have been successful selling beauty products or selling used items around the house or from yard sales on eBay.

If you are working more than two part-time jobs, be aware of each employer's expectations to avoid scheduling conflicts. Communicate with each employer up front and let them know you are trying to survive and pay the bills. Share your available times based on your schedule. That type of flexibility is one advantage of having multiple jobs. If one employer lays you off or can't work around your schedule, you still have other jobs as opposed to only having one full-time job that would leave you crippled financially if they laid you off.

Beware of getting burnt out from so many jobs. You can easily find yourself working seventy-hour weeks. Of course, if working this hard is part of your plan to pull yourself out of a financial rut, your hard work will eventually pay off.

As a sidebar, the part-time jobs could also help you avoid wage garnishment, because your income level could be considered too low to garnish.

Strategy #26
Down The
Corporate Ladder

Some people stay unemployed much longer than they have to because they refuse to take a job that pays less money or offers less status than they held at their previous job. I know it is difficult to settle for a $30,000 a year job when you have been accustomed to making $50,000 a year but if the unemployment checks will be running out soon and you still have not found a job equivalent to the one you lost, consider downsizing a bit and take that lower paying job.

If there is not much opportunity for growth at the new job, ask your new employer if you can work four ten-hour days instead of five eight-hour days. The extra day off will give you the opportunity to continue interviewing for a better position, while working the lower paid one to make ends meet.

So that you don't put all your eggs in one basket, consider part-timing it or finding a side hustle as mentioned in the previous strategies. This would provide you the extra flexibility needed while searching for that dream job.

Strategy #27
The Best Things In
Life Are Free

ork for free. That's right! You read correctly—work for free! Tell a potential employer to give you the opportunity to prove yourself by working FREE for two, four, or six weeks, or whatever time frame you are comfortable with, under one condition: if you perform well, they will hire you!

What do you have to lose if you're broke and unemployed anyway? Especially if you have been pounding the pavement for months on end with no luck. At least this way, after a short period of time, you will have a job.

Just make sure you get a written agreement that is signed and notarized. Be specific about your work duties, and potential salary and benefits. Also, put in a stipulation that your performance will be evaluated daily. This assures that there are no surprises if you are not hired, as well as giving you a better opportunity to see whether the potential employer would be a good fit.

While you are volunteering your time to prove yourself, make sure you keep a day or two free to continue the job search. It is also very important to make sure you present your work-for-free proposal to an employer who is actually hiring and not an employer who is just looking for free labor. Check the classified ads, and then contact potential employers with your proposition.

Strategy #28
"Well, We're Moving On Down!"

The price difference between having a two- or three-bedroom apartment can be as much as $300 per month. A good broke man strategy would be to make the switch. That is, if you live in a three-bedroom apartment, switch to a two-bedroom when your lease is up or move from a two-bedroom to a one-bedroom. You can even save money by moving from a one-bedroom to a studio.

If your financial situation is too grave to wait for your lease to end, talk to your landlord about your situation. You may be charged a small fee for breaking your lease, but still be allowed to make the switch. You can always move back up when things improve.

This is also a good strategy for college students. When a scholarship fell through, one student was able to move from a private dorm room to a shared dorm room. He lost his privacy and had to deal with a sloppy roommate, but was able to remain in college.

In cases of divorce or death of a spouse when you were relying on a spouse to help with the mortgage, you may consider selling your house and moving into a less expensive one while you still have equity built in your home. Many people take out second mortgages in an attempt to hold on to something they may eventually lose in the long run for the sake of nostalgia.

Strategy #29
Free Money?

===

Grants to individuals (especially students) are available from private foundations and the federal and state governments. These entities issue millions of dollars in grant money to a variety of individuals and groups each year. Grant programs are not loans. You decide how much you need and the money is yours to keep and doesn't have to be repaid. This grant money is non-taxable and interest-free! Grant programs don't require credit checks, collateral, security deposits, or co-signers, so you can apply even if you have bad credit.

Bookstores and the Internet are flooded with information and books for sale that promise hidden wealth. You end up purchasing an extensive list of foundations, government agencies, and private sources that provide these grants in various categories. But you are soon disappointed when you discover during your research that most of the funding sources have geographical boundaries. You may only come across a handful of possible sources that fit your needs based on locale, ethnicity, or grade point average and you are competing with hundreds of other people vying for the same funds!

That doesn't mean you shouldn't try. Miracles can happen. But instead of paying for the information, which is basically a list of names, addresses, and phone numbers, visit your local library or conduct research on the Internet for FREE. It will only cost you a little time and effort, but you will likely find more updated leads and increase your chances.

Free money is difficult to get, but with a lot of diligence and persistence, you just might get lucky.

Strategy #30
The Big Gamble

Y ou are tired of being broke. I know it's been an uphill battle and you want a quick way out. Spending a dollar a day on lottery tickets may seem like a harmless act. After all, it's only a dollar, right? Well, on the surface it may seem to make sense. We hear stories of people who spent their last dollar on a lottery ticket and won millions. But the hard truth is the odds of that happening are something like one out of 120 million!

Yet, many get excited believing that they *could* be that lucky person. It is great to believe in beating the odds and taking a chance, but there are better odds and chances to take: starting a small business, earning a degree or certificate in an employable field, or maybe, um…getting struck by lightning!

Over time, most people who play the lottery seeking quick riches often lose $150 to $500 a year. Chronic players lose thousands. Multiply this by five, ten, or fifteen years or more and the figures are astonishing. Add to that the interest that could have been accumulated from even the lowest interest bearing savings account, and you would have a better gamble with better odds. And if by some chance you win $10 on a scratch ticket here and there, your losses almost always outweigh your gains.

If you have a few dollars to spare and want to play for fun, that is okay. Heck, we waste more on credit card interest fees. But when you are a broke man, down on your luck, be careful not to view it as an investment strategy!

Another gamble to avoid is get-rich-quick ventures that claim: *Earn $10,000 in 30 days with a $200 investment!* These claims are usually just trying to push you into a pyramid scheme where your profit comes from recruiting more people to pay the same $200 you paid. They'll tell you to recruit fifty people in thirty days who are willing to pay $200 and you reach the top—the $10,000 is yours! Chances are if you are broke, you don't know fifty people willing to fork over $200!

Not only are pyramid schemes illegal, but the bottom usually falls out when new members cannot be recruited fast enough. You will more than likely be the one at the bottom, plus if you have $200 to spare it would be better spent toward the rent!

Strategy #31
Stop Hanging
With The Joneses

Your friend, Jane Doe Jones, shows up to the PTA meeting wearing $200 designer shoes and carrying a $800 handbag. She instantly becomes the center of attention, receiving compliments and admiration by all those around her.

Before you know it, Old Man Envy is tapping you on the shoulder, whispering, *"That should be you." "You can afford that." "You deserve that attention." "You look way better than her anyway."* The next thing you know, you're eagerly awaiting your next paycheck because you can't wait to blow it all on the same overpriced shoes or handbag in a feeble attempt to "keep up with the Joneses." That is, buying items you cannot afford in an attempt to impress others and yourself.

The consequence? It depends. Perhaps the rent is late, utilities are in jeopardy of disconnection, or there is little food in the house. Either way, it was a foolish decision. Live by this creed: If you can't afford it, DON'T BUY IT!

This may all sound like common sense, but you would be surprised at the number of people going through hard times who are making their situation worse by trying to keep up with the Joneses.

It's okay to want the finer things in life. That desire is what motivates many of us to become successful. However, if you cannot afford the finer things in life, but ignore this fact, you will only end up successfully broke! Don't let this be you!

Don't be fooled. The world is full of *Jones Wannabes*. You know — the ones who drive a BMW, but live in their parents' basement! Or that friend who meets you for lunch dressed head-to-toe in expensive designer clothing only to have the waiter come back to inform them that their credit card rejected their $8.00 lunch charge!

Most of those people you think are the Joneses are really just phonies. That's right, a lot of those society types you see driving luxury automobiles and wearing expensive clothing are virtually penniless. They live hand-to-mouth and spend their money before they get it.

Just watch some of these reality shows that draw attention to people with seemingly affluent lifestyles flaunting their "*wealth*" and later on you read about their foreclosures and bankruptcies. As a matter of fact, many of them are leasing their mansions and expensive cars. Why? Because they just can't afford the fancy homes and cars they flaunt.

Remember, the true Joneses are more than likely the people who are not living in extravagant homes or driving luxurious cars. They live modestly by following this simple rule: Spend less money than you earn and save as much money as you can along the way.

Strategy #32
A Slice of Humble Pie

erhaps you used to live the good life, complete with a high-paying job, nice home, luxury car, and a nice cushion saved in the bank. But out of nowhere the economy took a turn for the worse. Then, without warning, you get laid off work. Soon, you find yourself collecting unemployment benefits in an amount that doesn't come close to meeting your expenses.

But no, you do not want to adjust to the shift in tide. Your pride will not allow you to. Instead, you continue spending as if your life hasn't changed. Why? Because you want to keep up appearances? In the meantime, checks are bouncing and credit cards are being declined left and right. But you still refuse to let on that you are experiencing hardship. After all, what would people think?

Hopefully, this scenario does not apply to you, but if it does, then STOP IT! Now that you are going through hard times and trying to survive, life is different.

Sure, back in the good ole days you could afford to dine at fancy restaurants. Well, *back then* you could afford it. Now that you are trying to feed your family and keep the lights and gas on, your priorities should change. Trade in luxury for survival and call it a day. Now is the time to hold on to your resources and spend wisely.

Do not allow pride to entice you into buying things that you can no longer afford. Maybe your weekly visit to the hairdresser should be reduced to monthly or that flashy sports car needs to be traded for a used, compact car. Humility is the best way to prepare ourselves for the unexpected changes in life, so cut yourself a big slice of humble pie!

Strategy #33
Brother, Can You
Spare A Dime?

Many charitable organizations receive funding from government agencies and private foundations to provide rent, mortgage, utility assistance, and food vouchers to struggling families. Check with your local Catholic Charities, United Way, Continuum of Care, local municipal department or phone book for a list of social service organizations in your area that can help.

Assistance with childcare costs is also available for working mothers who meet certain income guidelines. Check with the Health and Human Services Department in your state for more information.

You may also qualify for county, state, and federally-funded employment training programs designed to help you get back on your feet. For instance, the Workforce Investment Act (WIA) provides Individual Training Accounts (ITA) to eligible adults and dislocated workers who are seeking a way to find rewarding employment in a skilled occupation.

ITAs are distributed through local WIA one-stop centers. These ITA vouchers are like financial aid that can be used at participating schools and training facilities (often referred to as training providers) that will provide you with the skills training you need over a short period of time. There are tons of training programs to choose from, such as Certified Nursing Assistant (CAN), Dental Hygienist, Truck Driving (CDL), or Network Cabling. The best part is that, if you qualify, this is all FREE OF CHARGE! This is a great opportunity to obtain the skills needed to obtain a high-paying job in a demand-driven industry.

Visit careeronestop.org to find an employment training site in your state or check with the Workforce

Investment Board in your area for a list of local service providers that are eager to lend you a helping
hand!

Strategy #34
Bill Payment Help

F ederal and state governments provide funding through various programs that can help you pay vital bills, such as past-due rent and utilities. Here are a few: **Emergency Shelter Grants (ESG)** has a homeless prevention component that provides funds to aid people who are at risk of becoming homeless due to eviction, foreclosure, or utility shutoff by paying first-month's rent, rent arrearages, and past-due utility payments.

FEMA does more than just help during national disasters. They also sponsor the **Emergency Food and Shelter Program (EFSP)** which was created to help people in need of emergency assistance. EFSP is utilized to assist individuals and families with issues regarding payment of utility bills, rent and mortgage payments, as well as temporary shelter and food.

The **Low Income Home Energy Assistance Program (LIHEAP)** is a federally-funded program that provides a once-per-year payment for heat (primary utility) and electric (secondary utility) to income-eligible applicants. The LIHEAP Program is able to provide once-a-year reconnection assistance payments for applicants whose utility has been disconnected for non-payment or applicants who are being denied service because of an old bill. LIHEAP is also able to provide emergency furnace repair or replacement for eligible applicants whose furnace does not work or is red-tagged by the utility company.

Weatherization Assistance Program (WAP) was created to help low-income families reduce their energy costs. The WAP program provides for home improvement in the form of insulating walls and ceilings, repairing broken windows, caulking and weatherproofing, and by replacing inefficient heating and cooling appliances.

Various social service agencies apply to federal and state governments to receive these funds and distribute to those who qualify within their service delivery areas.

Strategy #35
Homelessness Prevention

Many individuals and families lose their homes due to job loss or mortgages that ballooned into payments that were beyond their reach. As a result, many formally stable, middle-class families are facing homelessness. Fortunately, there are programs available to help families that are homeless or in danger of becoming homeless get back on their feet.

Most people think that housing assistance programs are only designed for specific populations such as veterans, long-term homeless persons with disabilities, serious mental illness, diseases or drug and substance abuse issues. However, you do not have to belong to any of those subpopulations to receive housing assistance through various HUD-sponsored programs. The definition of who can be considered homeless is found in Section 103 of the HUD McKinney-Vento Act and states: *"someone who is living on the street or in an emergency shelter, or <u>who would be</u> living on the street or in an emergency shelter without supportive housing assistance."* If you fit the definition, here are a few housing programs to consider:

Transitional Housing: This program's emphasis is to help transition individuals or families from homelessness to permanent housing in a short period of time by providing free temporary housing for women, men, and families. The stay in a transitional housing program can last anywhere from three to twenty-four months. They are designed to provide an opportunity to find work and get back on your feet while providing you with supportive services such as childcare and job training that can help you live in permanent housing again.

SECTION 8 Housing Choice Voucher Program: Managed by local Public Housing Authorities,

Section 8 is a program that provides affordable housing opportunities to low-income families and other special populations by providing housing vouchers. Section 8 has gotten a bad rap over the years mostly due to abuse of the program; however, many families use Section 8 responsibly as they work to improve their quality of life.

There are basic eligibility requirements for Section 8. The primary one is income. In most cases, the family's income may not exceed 50 percent of the median income for the county or metropolitan area in which the family chooses to live. The family is responsible for finding their own suitable housing and a landlord who will accept Section 8 vouchers. A housing subsidy is then paid directly to the landlord on behalf of the family. The family must pay the balance of the rent not covered by the voucher, which is usually 30 percent.

Section 8 Home Ownership Program: Participating Public Housing Authorities can allow eligible individuals and families to convert current Section 8 vouchers from rental subsidies to mortgage subsidies and purchase a modest home. This is available to first-time home buyers, but don't think you are out of the running because you have owned a home in the past. HUD's definition of a first-time home buyer is someone who has not owned or had an ownership interest in a residence for *the last three years.* You still have to meet income and employment requirements and at least one percent of the purchase price must come from personal resources. Other requirements include homeownership counseling and periodic housing inspections for as long as you are receiving assistance.

Whether you consider the Section 8 Housing Choice Voucher or the Home Ownership Program, the waiting list can take months or years depending on where you live. Contact the local Public Housing Authority in your area for more information.

Strategy #36
Leave The Lights On

A lot of corporate executives seek temporary lodging that provides them with a feeling of home while away on business. An upscale, furnished home can rent for upwards of $3,000 per month or more and there are large corporations who are able to foot the bill. This extra money can be used to pay your mortgage and possibly other bills.

While you are renting your home, move in with Mom and Dad or other relatives (*don't forget that slice of humble pie*). If living with relatives is not an option and your home is nice enough to charge a competitive rate, try renting a small apartment for yourself while your home is being used. To attract lodgers, place an ad in the newspaper and contact realtors and major corporations.

If renting your entire home is not possible, consider renting out a basement or spare room in your home. This is a great alternative if you are having trouble paying the bills.

Calculate your average monthly expenses and charge your roommate a lump sum equal to 55 or 60 percent of the total and profit a little. I think this is better than trying to go fifty-fifty on everything. After all, it is *your* place.

When on the lookout for a boarder, first try to find a reliable family member or friend. I know friends and relatives can sometimes be the worst tenants and often want a pass when the bills come due. Still, in today's world, it's better to personally know the person you live with than to live with a stranger. But, if friends or relatives just won't work, try a roommate-matching service. Just remember when dealing with strangers, don't slack on checking their references.

Strategy #37
An Attitude Of
Gratitude

I n a world of gadgets, gizmos, glitz, and glamour, it is easy to focus on what you do not have, but always try to find something to be grateful for. This is easier said than done, especially when everything around you seems to be falling apart. Being grateful can keep you in a positive state of mind, and optimism is crucial to surviving hard times.

Don't think you have anything to be grateful for? There is always a silver lining. For instance, maybe you are in good health. That's a blessing. Celebrate the fact that you have a roof over your head. Or better yet, be thankful for the fact that you have a sound mind that will help you get through this temporary shortfall. If you are breathing, there is no shortage of things you can feel grateful about.

Sit down and write a list of what you are grateful for or something good that happened to you each day. It could be something as simple as being called in for a job interview (whether you get the job or not). Or the bus driver who waited for you while you ran a block to catch the bus. Be grateful for all good things. This will make you conscious of the positive things happening around you and help take your focus away from the negative.

Another way to assure you have an attitude of gratitude is to surround yourself with positive people. When you surround yourself with people who are cheerful, ambitious, energetic, encouraging, and harmonious, you are likely to become the same way and feel better when you are around them.

On the other hand, negative people drain your energy. They are always complaining, criticizing, and condemning everyone around them. In short, they drain your energy and assist you in staying focused on the problems in your life. Misery loves company and if you are not careful, the misery might rub off on you. So, the minute you feel that urge to whip out that old guitar and sing the blues, stop and think of the positive things you have going on in your life, and start singing about how grateful you are for them instead.

Remember you are not the victim of your circumstances, but rather the controller of it. Don't harp on the mistakes you've made in life; be grateful for them. Learning from your mistakes helps you to grow. When you know better, you do better!

Strategy #38
Give A Little

W hen you are broke, the last thing on your mind is giving. Receiving sounds like the more appealing option, especially when your lists of needs are growing each day.

Many believe that giving is reserved for the wealthy and when they have more, that's when they will give. Others say it is not about what you give or how much you give, but *that* you give. The love you put into giving is where the true blessings lie. I tend to agree with the latter.

Here is a story about giving that I find inspiring: A single mother of three was headed to a corner store to buy groceries. She worked full-time as a nursing assistant, but barely earned enough money to provide for her family. On her journey, she saw a homeless man carefully picking through a bag of trash, searching for something to eat.

On her way back from the store, she saw the same man still searching, but now with a small pile of partially eaten food carefully placed on a torn piece of plastic from a garbage bag. Well, that just broke her heart. Without saying a word or thinking of her safety, she handed the man a loaf of bread, a package of bologna, and a container of apple juice from her bag.

The man's face lit up and he thanked her profusely as he opened the apple juice and drank as if he had been lost in a desert for days. As she walked away, she pondered why she would do such a thing. Not only was it potentially dangerous, but she had just given away her children's lunch!

Later that night, while sorting through her mail, a hundred dollar bill fell out onto her lap. She immediately summoned her children to find out who had taken the mail out of the mailbox and questioned them repeatedly about the money. None of her children knew anything. Finally, her seven-year-old said, "Mommy, I think your guardian angel sent it." She suddenly remembered her kind deed, and answered, "Sure did."

The moral of this story is not give a homeless person a loaf of bread and you'll get $100. The moral is when you give unconditionally from the heart, wonderful things can happen.

Giving does not always have to be financial. You can give your time through volunteering at a social service agency; spending time with an elderly neighbor or an elderly stranger at a nursing home; or maybe offer free babysitting to a single mom you know.

Again, what you give or how you give is not important. Only that you give.

Strategy #39
Do Whatcha Gotta Do

S ometimes going through hard times forces us to take drastic measures to keep food on the table. Now, this is not a suggestion that you rob a bank, although some people would rather rob a bank than do what is about to be suggested. Apply for public assistance (also known as welfare). Oh my!

For many people, this option is no big deal. As a matter of fact, many people have abused the system for years by relying on public assistance as a permanent means for survival.

The Personal Responsibility and Work Opportunity Reconciliation Act of 1996 has put an end to that by attaching limitations on how long one can receive public assistance and incorporating other initiatives such as Workfirst, which is designed to move financially struggling families to work.

Still, honest, hardworking people who have never needed public assistance in their life have a hard time accepting this option. TANF (Temporary Assistance for Needy Families) is a monthly cash assistance program for struggling families with children under the age of eighteen. The key word here is *temporary*. This is a viable option to help families get by until their situation improves, which is why the program was designed.

Another form of public assistance is food stamps, which enables low-income families to buy groceries with coupons and Electronic Benefits Transfer (EBT) cards.

Taking advantage of public assistance, if you qualify, is nothing to be ashamed of. J.K. Rowling was a single mom on welfare when she wrote the first Harry Potter book. J.K. Rowling knew her financial strains at that time were temporary and set out to make sure of it. As a matter of fact, after Ms. Rowling had written the first Harry Potter book, she was so broke that she could not afford to have it photocopied to send to various publishers for consideration. So what did she do? Well, she didn't give up — that's for sure! Ms. Rowling typed each manuscript individually (hundreds of pages) to send to publishers. Now that's willpower!

So, if you need temporary financial assistance to help you improve your life for you and your children, then do whatcha gotta do!

Strategy #40
Ain't Too Proud To Beg

sking strangers for money is a commonly used method of acquiring needed cash. However, there are more clever ways to attain money from strangers without standing in a busy intersection holding up a sign or panhandling.

Cyber begging is a new craze where people plead their case to strangers in the hopes of getting out of debt, paying for cosmetic surgery or, in the case of one lady, looking for someone to help her pay the attorney costs to sue the church next door to her house for making too much noise!

The cyber begging craze got popular when Karyn Bosnak convinced strangers to help pay off her $20,000 credit card debt! She created a website (*www.savekaryn.com*) and was able to pay off her hefty credit card debt in less than five months by getting people to donate money to help eliminate her debt via her website, as well as selling her personal items on eBay. She got national acclaim for her efforts and received more than two million hits on her website.

When $250,000 was needed in thirty days to save his house from foreclosure, actor Dustin Diamond created a website where he gave autographed t-shirts to people who donated $15 or $20 to his cause. In a short period of time, he raised enough money to save his house.

Critics say that cyber begging is taking the easy way out and people are just dodging responsibility. But will those critics offer you a place to stay if you become homeless?

If you want to give cyber begging a whirl, all you have to do is find a free website deal, an inexpensive web hosting service, and a PayPal account. Some websites to try are beglist.org, cyberbegging.org and cyberbeg.com.

Some people have even held debt reduction parties where friends and family bring free food, drinks, and money.

Karyn, Dustin, and many others weren't too proud to beg and you shouldn't be either.

Strategy #41
Avoid Moochers

L inda calls her friend Kathy to see whether she wants to see a movie. Kathy agrees. So, Linda suggests that they meet up at a local theater later that night. That's when the problems erupt. Kathy begins her Oscar-worthy performance. She sighs desperately and laments, "I don't think I can make it because my car isn't working."

Linda really wants to go to the movies but doesn't want to go alone. Against her better judgment, she drives miles out of her way to pick up Kathy. When they arrive at the movie and it is time to pay, Act II of Kathy's performance unfolds as she begins fumbling through her purse, frantically looking for invisible funds, and then finally announces that she completely forgot about a bill she just paid and doesn't have any money. (Yeah, right.)

Linda rolls her eyes in disgust, but reluctantly pays Kathy's admission into the movie. She also buys Kathy popcorn and a soda, and drives her back home. In the end, Linda has wasted a total of $25.00 on Kathy.

Linda, who is broke most of the time and living on a tight budget, has to cut back on lunch next week to make sure she has enough gas money to make it to work.

As usual, Kathy promises to pay Linda back, but Linda isn't going to hold her breath. Kathy has played this game with Linda throughout their friendship. You see, Kathy is a certified moocher!

These types of so-called friends will mooch off you forever if you let them. You know the type. They can't pitch in to pay for the pizza, but they always want a free slice. Or they come over and eat everything out of your refrigerator and leave you searching for food to eat the next day. The moocher always promises to pay you back "tomorrow," but tomorrow never comes.

So why do we keep them as friends? Because moochers usually have great personalities and are the life of the party, but they are milking you dry.

If you are already struggling financially, you don't need a moocher friend making things worse. However, the solution is not to stop hanging out with the moocher because, after all, they're fun to be around. You just have to abide by the moocher survival rules:

1.   Never invite a moocher to any event that requires money.

2.   Always visit a moocher at their home, not yours.

3.   Never loan a moocher any money.

4.   Remember the universal moocher repellent phrase: "Sorry, dude. I don't have it."

Strategy #42
Excess Baggage

==

This chapter is mostly dedicated to the single women who have unemployed boyfriends living with and off them. These dudes are just sitting around the house all day wasting electricity while the woman is out there working her fingers to the bone.

The kids have nothing to eat because the boyfriend and his friends have eaten everything, even the SpaghettiOs . What's worse, the utility and telephone bills have almost doubled since he moved in. To top it all off, when you come home from working your *second* job, the house is a mess and he has the audacity to complain because there is nothing left to eat!

Men like this are just excess baggage you do not need. You will never get your finances in order with a person like this holding you back. It is not good for you or the kids (if you have any).

If you must have an unemployed, live-in boyfriend, at least find one who would rather pound the pavement all day looking for a job than sit around your house all day.

However, this is not a problem exclusive to women. If you are a man who has a girlfriend who fits the description of excess baggage, kick her to the curb as well.

It is best to surround yourself with positive people who can contribute to your plan to make your life better, especially while you are broke. You can do bad all by yourself.

Strategy #43
To The Penny

E very penny counts, especially when you are broke. That's why one of the most important things to have when you are broke is a budget. It doesn't matter whether it's monthly, weekly, or daily. Spending must be tracked at all times.

Keep a little memo pad and write down every little thing you buy. At the end of the day, highlight all nonessential items purchased and tally them up. Seeing a tally of wasted money grow before your very eyes is a good deterrent to over-spending. Although people who are truly broke should not have any non-essential items to tally, people teetering on the borderline of "broke-ness" because of unwise spending will find this method to be a real eye-opener.

Another good way to prevent yourself from spending the money that is burning a hole in your pocket is to separate the money into envelopes and label them by category. For instance, if you have budgeted $30 for gas money for the week put it in an envelope and label it *gas money*. If you have set aside $100 to buy groceries, place it in an envelope and label it *groceries*.

Having large sums of money in your wallet may make it difficult to remember the money is earmarked to pay a variety of expenses. Before you know it, you're impulse buying and finding yourself without the money that was allotted to pay an important bill. However, if the money is already separated into various envelopes labeled for its purpose, you can easily take each envelope as needed. Therefore, you will be less likely to buy that new shirt with money from an envelope marked *"electric bill"*!

Regardless of what your tracking method is, you must keep a close eye on what money comes in and goes out. Make sure that you are always able to pay those priority bills!

Strategy #44
Be A Cheapskate

When going through hard times, finding creative ways to cut corners in your budget becomes an art form. Small changes can make a considerable difference. Here are a few examples of ways to give your budget some wiggle room. These simple strategies could equate to a 20 percent saving on your monthly budget.

MEALS: Plan meals in advance and shop according to the items you need to prepare the meals for the week. And never go to the grocery store without a shopping list or you might find yourself throwing all sorts of unnecessary items into your shopping cart. Also, cook one-pot meals such as casseroles, soups, and slow cooker meals. They are a guaranteed way to ensure there is enough for seconds and leftovers for another day.

You might be tired of hearing about coupons, but they are a real money saver. Try planning your meals around coupons and weekly sales. It will save you a bundle. With the Internet, you don't have to buy the local paper to find coupons anymore. Check websites like Coupons.com and GroceryCoupons4U.com for the items you purchase.

CLOTHING: Buy your clothing off-season. September-November is a great time to rack up on summer clothes that are on clearance for as much as 80 percent off! Likewise, January-February is usually a great time to rack up on winter clothes. When shopping for children's clothing, don't just check those clearance racks for clothing in their current size. Think about next year or even the year after. And always be on the lookout for unused or gently used clothing at thrift stores and garage sales.

UTILITIES: Save on energy costs by unplugging unused appliances and turning off lights in empty rooms. Spare the AC for dangerous heat waves and crack a window on a breezy day. Also, wear comfy long sleeves, long pants, and socks with slippers at home during the winter months and turn down the heat a notch. You can also save on water by limiting showers to five or ten minutes and turning off the water while you brush your teeth. These are simple changes that could go a long way.

OTHER TIPS: Be on the alert for back-to-school freebies. Many community organizations and churches provide free school supplies. Also, stock up on great sale items such as toilet paper and canned goods. Finally, beware of those stores with the word "dollar" attached to them. They don't always have the best deals. Make sure you know your prices.

Strategy #45
Keep Your Cool

L iving the life of a broke man is a difficult experience. It could easily damage your self-esteem and possibly cause depression. In order to survive this situation, you must have a positive attitude and smile your way through this temporary adversity.

For instance, seeking public assistance is tough for many of us, especially when you have never had to in the past. The experience becomes even worse when you find yourself at the public aid office for hours waiting for your name to be called.

The situation only worsens and becomes more humiliating when, after your long wait, you find yourself sitting in front of a rude, insensitive, overworked case manager who appears to have little empathy for your situation. Although you are tempted to give the ill-mannered case manager a piece of your mind, DON'T DO IT! Instead, be kind, patient, and leave with a smile and a thank-you. Even if they didn't deserve it!

Circumstances have forced you into hard times. You are not alone. Millions of people are suffering along with you! Some people will survive hard times and get back on their feet, while others may struggle through hard times for the rest of their lives. Why? Because some people choose to fight their way through hardship, while others tuck in their tails and stay in it. The best weapon you have to fight with is a positive attitude. It doesn't cost a thing and no one can take it away from you!

So, keep your head up and do your best with what you have. Remember, trouble doesn't last always.

Strategy #46
If It Ain't Nailed Down, Sell It!

===

G randma Margie's husband of forty years died without a life insurance policy, but that didn't bother her. She knew that she and her husband were not rich. Instead, Grandma Margie took comfort in knowing that the home they lived in for nearly forty years was paid in full. That is, until she received a notice of foreclosure. She soon discovered that her husband had taken out a second mortgage without her knowledge and nearly $10,000 was still owed on their home. She did not have the money needed to save her house from foreclosure.

Grandma Margie was well-liked in her church and community. So, when the word got around about her dilemma, many fundraisers were held on her behalf. These efforts helped her raise close to $6,000. With approximately $4,000 needed and not much time to spare, Grandma Margie decided to have an "Antique Garage Sale." She sold most everything she owned, including a vintage automobile that once belonged to her late husband. Her efforts paid off and she raised more than enough money to save her home, but lost all of her cherished keepsakes in the process.

When word got around about what Grandma Margie had done, her story made the local news. She was interviewed in her home that housed only a bed, a chair, and a small table. Soon, many of the people who purchased items from Grandma Margie began to return them to her. She also received monetary gifts and furniture from all over the state.

Although Grandma Margie's end result was unique, selling items that she owned in an attempt to keep a roof over her head was a clever strategy.

Hopefully, your situation does not warrant your selling *everything* you own. But having a garage sale or selling a few cherished items on eBay in order to keep food on the table is not shameful—it's survival. Material things can always be replaced.

Strategy #47
Go Find Big Momma

S ometimes you need a dose of tough love to get back on track. In the African American family, Big Momma or Madea is the old school matriarch and stern disciplinarian of the family. When you are scurrying down the wrong path, Big Momma is usually the first person to call attention to the error of your ways and give you that swift kick on the back side as a friendly reminder.

You won't find Big Momma coddling you when you mess up. You won't hear Big Momma say, "Oh sweetie...it's okay...woe is you..." You're more likely to feel a wet dish rag smacked against your head and hear her yelling, "Stop sitting around here moping all day! You're not the first person to get knocked down by life! Pull yourself together and get back in the race!"

Your Big Momma doesn't have to be your grandmother; she can be anyone whose opinion you trust and respect such as a spouse, a relative, a friend, a coach or a teacher. She can be anyone who loves you enough to hurt your feelings for your own good.

We often surround ourselves with people who will let us fall on our face without a word of caution either because they are afraid to lose us as a friend or maybe just don't care. When you are broke and struggling to make it, these people help you stay in a broke state of mind. You need someone who cares enough about you to douse you with a bucket of ice water while you are sleeping in the middle of a Monday afternoon and yell, "Get your butt out of bed and go find a job!"

Strategy #48
Ain't Nobody's Business

D on't go around telling every-body your business! There's no need to walk around all willy-nilly, com-plaining to everybody that you are going through hard times. *"I just don't know how I am going to make it." "I can barely make ends meet." "Woe is me."*

This is not to say that you should ignore the fact that you are going through hard times, because you have to recognize trouble to change it. Just don't harp on it and constantly talk about your personal business all day, every day to anyone and everyone who will listen.

If you just have to talk about it and get it out of your system, find a confidant—that one person you can trust who won't repeat your personal business. But after you spill your guts, let that be the end of it. Get it out and let it go!

If it's a serious matter that requires professional counseling, find someone qualified to talk to. Many social service agencies offer free counseling. If you are a member of a church, perhaps you could speak with your pastor.

Not only should you stay away from telling *your* personal business, you should also not tell *other people's* business. Everybody loves to hear juicy gossip—until it's about them!

Unfortunately, there are people eager to gossip about the fact that you are going through hard times, especially if you were once doing well. So, don't give them any ammunition. It is your personal business and you are entitled to privacy.

As a sidebar, if you don't want people to know you shop at a thrift store (*though there is nothing wrong with it*), then shop at a thrift store in another community. If you would rather your neighbors not know

153

you are using food vouchers, then go outside your neighborhood to use them. You get the point. It ain't nobody's business what you do!

Strategy #49
Fake It
Until You Make It

enry Ford is noted for the saying, "Think you can or think you can't. Either way you are right!" His point is that if you think you can succeed and achieve greatness, then you will, but if you think you can't, then the end is as ominous as you think it will be.

Sometimes it is difficult for a broke man to believe he or she can do better and pull themselves out of the gutter of hard times. There is no magic button to push that will instantly put you in the mindset of success but there is a magic solution: Fake it until you make it!

There was a lady who worked in corporate America for years and found herself out of work. After months of looking for a new job, she was unsuccessful. One day, she was in the park, walking her sister's four dogs, when she was approached by someone who asked her how much she charged to walk dogs.

She could have explained that her sister was recovering from major surgery and she was just helping out, but instead she blurted out, "Twenty dollars," and instantly got her first customer. She quickly had business cards made and posted flyers in her sister's building and her dog walking business was born. She did not have the experience, but she faked it. Her business grew to include four employees and a menu of other services for dogs.

Say you don't have the confidence to complete a specific task at hand. Fake what you do not know. Put yourself out there. Tell yourself you can complete the task at hand as well as anyone can and get it done. It won't be perfect at first as you feel your way through. Before you know it, faking it will become authentic. You will soon believe you can make it and that, my friend, is all the ammunition you need!

Strategy #50
The Broke Man's Plan

J uggling bills and stretching a dollar until it screams should be a temporary way of life. Although living on a budget is important in any income bracket, we all want to get to the point where our budgets are large enough for us to live comfortably without fear or worry. So, in the midst of all the money crunching, there should be a plan in the works to put an end to the commonly used Robbing Peter to Pay Paul budget.

But then again, you can't just sit around *hoping* and *wishing* for your finances to improve. You must have a plan—not just one plan, but a Plan A, a Plan B, a Plan C, and maybe even a Plan D, E, and F! Most people just need a little time to pull themselves out of a financial rut. So, devise a plan that will help you get back on your feet.

For example, if you have just been laid off, Plan A might be to get another job that pays a wage equal or greater than your previous job. If after a month you're still looking for work, you may need to resort to Plan B. Plan B might be to take a job that is not exactly what you were looking for, but what you can get for now. Plan C might be to take some free courses in a career field that is in demand *while* you work for that job you settled for in Plan B.

There is no perfect plan. You must design one that fits your personality, needs, and circumstances. For instance, do not plan to become a nurse if you faint at the sight of blood. Or do not open a daycare center if you do not much like being around kids. But there are plenty of options available to you. Go to your local community college and take an aptitude test. That might help steer you in the right direction.

Need help developing a plan? Meet with a career counselor or a job developer to help you. Most counties have one-stop centers funded by the Workforce Investment Act (WIA). These programs will not only help you develop an Individual Service Strategy (*a sophisticated word for existing plan*) that will help you reach your goals, but also pay for skills training.

Some people might be able to get back on their feet after Plans A, B, or C, while others might need a Plan Q, R, & S before they get their lives back on track. It doesn't matter how many times you have to pick yourself up and dust yourself off. All that matters is that you have a road map to follow into a better financial situation.

Afterword

here you have it—50 Broke Man's Survival Strategies. Use the Broke Man's Survival Strategies at your discretion to buy yourself the time you need to pull your finances together.

This guide was not trying to be all things to all people. It was developed for people with good intentions who have just fallen into a bad situation and just trying to survive. Some of you reading this guide could relate to the material covered because you either have "been there" or "are there."

Still, I am sure there will be many critics of this guide. Most will be people who have never been broke or been in a financial situation so dark that it seems impossible to ever see daylight and are oblivious of the broke man's plight.

At any rate, whether you utilize the nontraditional methods listed in this guide to survive your temporary financial dilemma or more traditional methods like credit counselors or bankruptcy attorneys, everyone must do what they think is best to solve their individual financial crisis. Either way, I hope in some way you found this guide helpful.

Good Luck!

A.M. Harris

References

Fair Debt Collection Practices Act

http://www.federalreserve.gov/boarddocs/supmanual/cch/fairdebt.pdf

Making Home Affordable

http://www.makinghomeaffordable.gov/pages/default.aspx

WIA Career One Stop

http://www.careeronestop.org/WiaProviderSearch.asp

Home Business Ideas

http://www.2work-at-home.com/ideas.shtml

FEMA: Emergency Food and Shelter Program

https://www.efsp.unitedway.org/efsp/website/index.cfm or

http://www.fema.gov/public-assistance-local-state-tribal-and-non-profit/recovery-directorate/emergency-food-shelter

Low Income Home Energy Assistance Program

http://www.acf.hhs.gov/programs/ocs/programs/liheap

Weatherization Assistance Program

http://www1.eere.energy.gov/wip/wap.html

HUD Public Housing

http://portal.hud.gov/hudportal/HUD?src=/program_offices/public_indian_housing

Temporary Assistance to Needy Families

http://www.acf.hhs.gov/programs/ofa/programs/tanf

Free Counseling

http://contactcrisisline.org/